PRAYERSCRIPTS
Speaking God's Word Back to Him

"BRETHREN, PRAY FOR US" ➤➤

ADVANCING THE WORD OF GOD

31 Days of Prophetic Intercession to
SEE GOD'S WORD MULTIPLY, PREVAIL, AND TRANSFORM LIVES

CYRIL OPOKU

Advancing the Word of God: 31 Days of Prophetic Intercession to See God's Word Multiply, Prevail, and Transform Lives

Published by *Quest Publications*

ISBN: 978-1-988439-88-4

Cover design by *Quest Publications (questpublications@outlook.com)*

Unless otherwise indicated, all Scripture quotations are taken from the World English Bible WEB, which is in the public domain. For more information, visit: www.worldenglish.bible

This book is a work of devotional encouragement. It is not intended to replace biblical study, pastoral counsel, or professional therapy.

Printed in the United States of America.

First Edition: September 2025

For more books like this, visit *PrayerScripts:* https://prayerscripts.org

CONTENTS

Contents..iii

Dedication...v

Preface vi

How to Use This Book...viii

Introduction..xi

WEEK 1: FOUNDATIONS FOR THE INCREASE OF GOD'S WORD 1

Day 1: Faithful to the Ministry of the Word 3

Day 2: Swift Progress of the Gospel 5

Day 3: Bold Utterance of the Gospel 7

Day 4: The Word Multiplied and Prevails 9

Day 5: Fruit-Bearing Power of the Gospel 11

Day 6: The Sure Fulfillment of God's Word..............................13

Day 7: Commissioned to Disciple Nations 15

WEEK 2: BOLDNESS AND GROWTH AMID PERSECUTION 17

Day 8: Fearless in Opposition..19

Day 9: Chains for the Gospel's Advance......................................21

Day 10: The Word Is Not Bound...23

Day 11: Scattered But Unstoppable...25

Day 12: Unashamed of the Gospel...27

Day 13: Treasure in Earthen Vessels 29

Day 14: Prayer for Unity and Boldness...31

WEEK 3: BY SIGNS AND WONDERS, CONFIRMING THE WORD............................33

Day 15: Boldness and Heavenly Power..35

Day 16: Speaking Boldly in Grace...37

Day 17: Triumph Over False Powers 39

Day 18: Signs Following the Preached Word 41

Day 19: Authority Over Serpents and Darkness..........................43

Day 20: God Also Bearing Witness..45

Day 21: The God of Signs..47

WEEK 4: OVERCOMING OPPOSITION THROUGH SPIRITUAL WARFARE................ 49

Day 22: An Open Door Amid Adversaries.. 51

Day 23: Chains Broken by Prayer... 53

Day 24: Strengthened in the Armor of God................................... 55

Day 25: Mighty Through God.. 57

Day 26: Resisting the Enemy 59

Day 27: Strengthened by Heavenly Visitation............................. 61

Day 28: Overcoming by the Blood... 63

Day 29: Wielding the High Praises.. 65

Day 30: Treading on Serpents and Scorpions 67

Day 31: Eyes Opened to See Victory.. 69

Epilogue 71

Encourage Others with Your Story.. 73

More from PrayerScripts.. 74

DEDICATION

This book is lovingly and prayerfully dedicated to the pastors who have shaped my Christian journey in ways words can scarcely capture:

To REV. (RTD) FRANCIS NYARKO—it was under your preaching that I first heard the voice of Christ calling me. Your unwavering passion for souls and your faithful oversight laid the foundation of my walk with God. Through your ministry, I learned not only to know the Lord but also to serve His church with reverence and joy.

To the late REV. JOSEPH OSEI-AMOAH—your mentorship marked a turning point in my life. You saw potential in me long before I saw it in myself. Under your guidance, I stepped into church leadership for the first time and began the journey of ministerial training. Though you have joined the cloud of witnesses, your legacy of faith and discipleship continues to live on in me.

To REV. ISAAC DE-GRAFT TAKYI—you opened my eyes to the spiritual gift of leadership and were the first to commission me to serve as a pastor. Your belief in me, your encouragement, and your push toward deeper theological study have forever shaped my calling and ministry path.

This work is a tribute to your spiritual labor, love, and lasting impact on my life.

PREFACE

There are moments in life when God places a holy burden upon the heart that cannot be ignored. This book is a product of tears, groanings, and countless hours of prayer for pastors, missionaries, and Gospel carriers who labor on the frontlines. Time and again, I have sensed the Spirit whispering: *"Call My people back to intercession. Teach them to contend for the advancement of My Word."*

For years, I prayed mostly for personal needs and immediate circumstances. But the Lord began to stretch me beyond myself, reminding me that His Kingdom agenda is bigger than any individual concern. He opened my eyes to see that every sermon preached, every missionary sent, and every soul saved is upheld by unseen prayer. Behind every story of revival is a hidden army of intercessors who refused to be silent.

This book is a response to that call. It is an invitation for you to take your place in that hidden army. Each prayer has been crafted not as a formula, but as a prophetic script to help you align with God's heartbeat. As you pray through these pages, I believe the Spirit will awaken fresh fire in you—not only to lift up your own pastor, but to join in global intercession for the unstoppable advance of God's Word.

I do not present this lightly. These prayers carry weight. They are not for spectators, but for those who are willing to step into the trenches of spiritual battle. If you are ready to see the Word multiply and prevail, then welcome—this journey is yours to embrace.

Advancing the Word of Life,
Cyril O. *(Toronto, September 2025)*

How to Use This Book

This book is designed as a daily companion to guide you into a prophetic lifestyle of prayer. This is a prayer journey meant to position you to walk in the fullness of God's promises. Here's how to make the most of it:

1. Dedicate a Daily Time:

Set aside a consistent time each day to engage with the prayer for that day. Treat this as sacred time with God, where distractions are minimized, and your heart is fully focused on communion with Him. Ten to twenty minutes daily is sufficient to meditate on the Scripture, pray, and receive revelation.

2. Begin with Scripture Reflection:

Each day begins with a carefully selected Scripture. Read it slowly, meditate on its meaning, and let the Holy Spirit illuminate how it applies to your life. Allow the Word to penetrate your spirit and prepare you to pray from a place of faith and expectancy.

3. Pray the Guided Prayer:

Use the prayer provided as a framework, allowing it to resonate with your own words and personal circumstances. Speak each declaration with authority and confidence, fully believing that God is at work. You may also pause to personalize the prayer for your specific family, career, or ministry needs.

- **Make It Personal**

  These prayers are written in the first person so you can make them your own. Speak them aloud, inserting the names of your family members, your workplace, your church, or your city where applicable. The more you personalize the prayer, the more you will sense its power shaping your reality.

- **Pray with Authority**

  These are not timid requests; they are bold decrees. Lift your voice as a covenant child of God, covered by the blood of Jesus and backed by heaven's authority. When you pray, do so with confidence that Christ has already won the victory on your behalf.

- **Leave Room for the Holy Spirit**

  These written prayers are a guide, not a limit. As you pray, pause to listen. The Holy Spirit may give you prophetic words, insights, or specific instructions. Follow His lead. Allow Him to expand the prayer, add declarations, or guide you into deeper intercession.

4. Journal Your Insights:

Keep a notebook or journal to record any thoughts, revelations, or confirmations you receive during prayer. Writing down what God speaks to you helps solidify understanding and creates a record of breakthrough and growth over time.

5. Repeat as Needed:

Some prayers or themes may need to be revisited multiple times. Answer to prayer is progressive; the more you engage with these prayers in faith, the greater the manifestation in your life and household. You can return to this book at any season to reinforce your victory and dominion.

6. Live in Expectancy:

Prayer is only one part of walking in enlargement—your actions, faith, and obedience amplify the power of these prayers. Move boldly into opportunities, embrace the doors God opens, and live with a confident expectation that God is answering your prayer beyond what you can see or imagine.

By following this guide daily, you will cultivate a lifestyle of prayer and kingdom impact. Let this book be your companion as you step into the new dimensions God has destined for you.

INTRODUCTION

Prayer has never been optional for the Church—it is the very lifeline through which the Word of God multiplies, prevails, and transforms lives. Wherever the Gospel has advanced throughout history, it has been carried on the wings of intercession. When the early believers gathered in upper rooms, their prayers ignited revival. When apostles faced persecution, their petitions shook prison doors open. When opposition arose, prayer released angelic assistance, boldness, and miracles that confirmed the Word. Every movement of God has been born in prayer, sustained in prayer, and expanded through prayer.

This book, *Brethren, Pray for Us: Advancing the Word of God*, is a call to join in that same unbroken chain of intercession. It is more than a devotional—it is a prophetic prayer journey designed to align your heart with God's eternal purpose for His Word. Over 31 days, you will be guided into Spirit-led, Scripture-rooted intercession for pastors, missionaries, and Gospel ministers around the world. Your voice, joined with countless others, becomes part of the global cry for the Word of the Lord to run swiftly and be glorified.

Inside, you will find carefully chosen Scriptures that emphasize the unstoppable power of God's Word in the face of trials, persecution, and opposition. Each day provides a prophetic prayer script that lifts your focus beyond personal needs and into Kingdom advance. You will intercede for boldness in preaching, for supernatural signs confirming the Word, for divine provision and open doors, and for protection against spiritual warfare.

Expect to be stirred. Expect your prayers to take on prophetic weight. Expect to see your intercession join Heaven's agenda in ensuring that God's Word multiplies and transforms lives. As you pray, you are not only standing for your pastor or church, but you are standing with the global Church, pressing forward the mission of Christ.

This is your invitation: step into the place of prayer, and watch as the Word of God runs, prevails, and reshapes nations.

WEEK 1: FOUNDATIONS FOR THE INCREASE OF GOD'S WORD

Every great movement of God begins in hidden places of prayer, surrender, and obedience. Before the Word spreads across nations, it first finds a home in consecrated hearts that yield to the Spirit's leading. Foundations matter. If a house is to stand tall and endure storms, its base must be firm; likewise, if the Word of God is to multiply and prevail, the people of God must lay a foundation of prayer, faithfulness, and divine dependence.

This week, we enter into a holy alignment with Heaven's blueprint. The Scriptures guiding us emphasize prayer that births provision, divine guidance that orders steps, and appointments prepared by God for the Word to flourish. We see the early Church committing themselves not to human strategies, but to prayer and the ministry of the Word. Their growth did not come by chance; it was the fruit of intentional devotion to the Lord's presence and His calling.

Our prayers will center on the provision of God—both spiritual and material—necessary for the advancement of His Word. We will intercede for divine guidance, asking the Lord to direct pastors, missionaries, and Gospel laborers into fruitful fields of ministry. We will also call forth divine appointments, moments orchestrated by Heaven where the Word meets hearts ready to receive.

By laying these foundations, we partner with God in preparing the soil for multiplication. We do not merely desire to see the Word spread; we long to see it rooted deeply, built securely, and flourishing continually. The story of Acts reminds us that when prayer and the Word take first place, growth is inevitable. This week, we establish that foundation through prophetic prayer, preparing the way for God's Word to increase without measure.

DAY 1

FAITHFUL TO THE MINISTRY OF THE WORD

"The twelve summoned the multitude of the disciples and said, 'It is not appropriate for us to forsake the word of God and serve tables. But we will continue steadfastly in prayer and in the ministry of the word.' The word of God increased and the number of the disciples multiplied in Jerusalem exceedingly. A great company of the priests were obedient to the faith."
—Acts 6:2, 4, 7 WEB

Righteous Father, I lift my voice in holy intercession today, declaring that Your Word is living and active, sharper than any two-edged sword, and destined to multiply in power. I stand in the gap for my pastor and the ministers You have set over Your people. Strengthen them, O Lord, to remain steadfast in prayer and fully committed to the ministry of the Word, without distraction or weariness. May their hearts be anchored in Your divine call, knowing that Your Word will never return void.

I cry out that every hindrance that seeks to drain their time, energy, or devotion be scattered by Your fire. Raise up faithful hands and hearts to support them, so that they can devote themselves to preaching, teaching, and interceding with fresh fire and unbroken focus. Release over them the mantle of wisdom and the anointing of prayer that breaks through principalities and powers.

Lord, I decree multiplication as it was in Jerusalem. Let the Word preached by my pastor pierce the hearts of multitudes, bringing conviction, repentance, and obedience to the faith. Cause the Gospel to run swiftly through the congregation and the city, increasing in fruitfulness. Let hardened hearts become fertile ground where Your Word can take deep root.

I declare, Father, that priests, leaders, and those in high places will be touched by the ministry of Your servants. Just as entire communities were shaken in the book of Acts, let a great company in this generation bow in obedience to Christ. May the testimony of increase be heard in every nation, city, and household where Your Word is proclaimed.

Empower Your ministers with grace to endure, faith to prevail, and boldness to release heaven's message without compromise. As they labor, may the Word of God multiply exceedingly until entire nations are discipled, and revival floods the earth.

In Jesus' name, Amen.

DAY 2

SWIFT PROGRESS OF THE GOSPEL

"Finally, brothers, pray for us, that the word of the Lord
may spread rapidly and be glorified, even as also with you."
—2 Thessalonians 3:1 WEB

Lord of the Harvest, I decree that this is the hour for Your Word to
run with speed and power across the earth. I lift up my pastor and
every minister You have anointed for this season. Let the Gospel
flow from their mouths unhindered, advancing swiftly into every
home, city, and nation You have appointed. May the Word not only
spread rapidly but be glorified, producing transformation and
testimonies that magnify the name of Jesus.

Father, breathe upon their ministry so that every word released
from the pulpit carries the weight of heaven. Cause the preached
Word to be received not as the word of man, but as the very Word
of God working effectively in those who believe. Remove every
delay, resistance, and barrier that slows down the progress of the
Gospel. I decree divine acceleration over the ministry of my
pastor—what took years shall now take months, what took months
shall now take days.

I intercede for the global Church, that ministers everywhere be
clothed with strength to labor tirelessly in prayer and the Word. Let
evangelists, teachers, and prophets be carriers of Your fire, releasing
a sound that awakens nations. Let the Word not only spread but be
glorified—exalted, honored, and received with reverence. May its

fruit be revival in the streets, holiness in homes, and salvation in the hearts of multitudes.

Father, raise up intercessors who will continually cry out for the swift progress of Your Word. Just as rivers rush with unstoppable force, let the Gospel overflow borders and languages, sweeping souls into Your Kingdom. Let the testimony of Your servants be that the Word of the Lord spread rapidly and was glorified everywhere they went.

In Jesus' name, Amen.

DAY 3

BOLD UTTERANCE OF THE GOSPEL

"Pray for me, that utterance may be given to me in opening my mouth, to make known with boldness the mystery of the Good News, for which I am an ambassador in chains; that in it I may speak boldly, as I ought to speak."
—Ephesians 6:19-20 WEB

Mighty God, I call on You today for my pastor and every minister of the Gospel around the world. Clothe them with holy boldness as ambassadors of the Kingdom. Grant them divine utterance so that every time they open their mouths, the mysteries of Christ are revealed with clarity, power, and conviction. Let no fear, intimidation, or opposition silence their voices. Instead, fill their spirits with courage to declare Your truth in every season.

I declare that chains, whether physical, spiritual, or circumstantial, will not hinder their witness. Just as Paul proclaimed Christ while imprisoned, so shall Your servants today preach unashamedly, even in the face of hostility. Strengthen them to carry the Good News into places of darkness, bringing light where hope has been lost.

Father, release an anointing of utterance over my pastor that pierces through spiritual blindness. Let words spoken from the pulpit carry prophetic weight, opening hearts and transforming lives. May they speak with precision and heavenly wisdom, addressing the needs of the people while revealing the eternal riches of Christ.

Raise up a generation of fearless preachers who will not compromise the truth for favor or comfort. Let the message of the cross thunder through nations, confronting sin, healing brokenness, and exalting Jesus Christ. Empower them, Lord, to speak as oracles of God, igniting revival wherever they are sent.

I decree that the voice of Your Word will not be silenced. As Your servants stand as ambassadors, let heaven back their every declaration with signs, wonders, and demonstrations of power. Through their boldness, may multitudes come to salvation, and the Kingdom of God advance without restraint.

In Jesus' name, Amen.

DAY 4

THE WORD MULTIPLIED AND PREVAILS

"When the Gentiles heard this, they were glad and glorified the word of God. As many as were appointed to eternal life believed. The Lord's word was spread abroad throughout all the region."
—Acts 13:48-49 WEB

Everlasting Father, I lift my voice in faith and decree that the Word released through my pastor and Your servants across the nations shall be received with gladness. As it was among the Gentiles, let every heart that hears the Gospel be filled with joy and reverence, glorifying Your Word. May many be appointed unto eternal life and believe, bringing great increase to the Body of Christ.

Lord, let every sermon preached, every prayer released, and every declaration made by Your ministers carry the fragrance of heaven. May entire regions be saturated with the Word, until no city, no village, no home remains untouched. Scatter the seed of the Word like holy fire, burning away unbelief and igniting faith wherever it goes.

Father, I decree that discouragement will not weaken Your ministers. Instead, joy shall fill their hearts as they witness multitudes respond with gladness. Give them grace to endure seasons of sowing and boldness to keep declaring the truth until the harvest bursts forth. Let those appointed to salvation be drawn irresistibly by the power of Your Spirit.

I call forth a regional awakening, Lord. Just as the Word spread through all of Asia, so let it cover the regions of our time. Let cities become centers of revival, nations become fields of harvest, and continents resound with testimonies of salvation. May the Word prevail over every demonic agenda and false philosophy.

Empower my pastor and every minister with fresh fire to proclaim the Word without ceasing. Let the global Church witness exponential growth as the Word of God spreads and multiplies beyond measure.

In Jesus' name, Amen.

DAY 5

FRUIT-BEARING POWER OF THE GOSPEL

"Which has come to you, even as it is in all the world and
is bearing fruit and growing, as it does in you also, since
the day you heard and knew the grace of God in truth."
—Colossians 1:6 WEB

Glorious God, I decree that Your Word shall not lie dormant but
will bear fruit and grow in the lives of those who hear it. I lift up my
pastor and Your ministers everywhere, that their labor in the Word
would release a harvest of transformed lives. Let the Gospel that has
come to us also move through us, producing good fruit in every
sphere of life.

Lord, just as the Colossians received and grew in the knowledge of
Your grace, let the people under my pastor's care grow into
maturity, walking in the fullness of Christ. Cause the Word to
flourish in families, marriages, businesses, and communities. May
the fruit of love, holiness, and faith abound.

Father, let the Gospel's expansion not be limited. Spread it to all
nations, bearing fruit across cultures and languages. Raise up
ministers who will not only sow but also water faithfully, so that
You, O Lord, give the increase. Empower the Word to penetrate
hearts deeply, uprooting sin and planting righteousness.

I decree that my pastor's ministry shall be marked by fruitfulness. Souls will be saved, disciples will be raised, and leaders will be equipped. Let the fruit of their labor remain and multiply, reproducing over generations.

May the testimony of the global Church echo this truth: the Gospel has come, is bearing fruit, and is growing in all the world. Father, let no ground remain barren. Let every nation taste and see the power of Your grace revealed through the Word.

In Jesus' name, Amen.

DAY 6

THE SURE FULFILLMENT OF GOD'S WORD

"For as the rain comes down and the snow from the sky, and doesn't return there, but waters the earth, and makes it grow and bud, and gives seed to the sower and bread to the eater; so is my word that goes out of my mouth: it will not return to me void, but it will accomplish that which I please, and it will prosper in the thing I sent it to do."
—Isaiah 55:10-11 WEB

Sovereign Lord, I declare with boldness that Your Word is unstoppable and unfailing. As rain waters the earth and causes life to flourish, so shall every word spoken through my pastor and Your ministers prosper in its assignment. I decree that not one word will return empty, but each shall accomplish the purpose for which it is released.

Father, let the preaching of Your Word be like rain upon thirsty ground. May it water dry hearts, awaken hope in the weary, and bring forth fruit where there has been barrenness. Let every sermon, teaching, and prophetic declaration carry divine life, producing seed for sowing and bread for nourishment.

I intercede that my pastor and ministers worldwide will not grow weary in releasing Your Word, even when results seem hidden. Assure them, O God, that the Word always prospers. Strengthen their faith that what is sown in tears will return in joy.

Lord, I decree supernatural harvests wherever Your Word is sent. In homes, may reconciliation spring forth. In cities, may righteousness be established. In nations, may revival break out. Let the Word prosper in healing, deliverance, and salvation, uprooting every lie of the enemy.

I call forth courage for ministers to speak what You command, even when unpopular, knowing that Your Word carries its own power to fulfill itself. Let confidence rise in their hearts that Your decrees cannot fail. Father, glorify Your name by fulfilling every word spoken in alignment with Your will.

In Jesus' name, Amen.

DAY 7

COMMISSIONED TO DISCIPLE NATIONS

> "Go and make disciples of all nations, baptizing them in
> the name of the Father and of the Son and of the Holy
> Spirit, teaching them to observe all things that I
> commanded you. Behold, I am with you always, even to
> the end of the age." Amen.
> —Matthew 28:19-20 WEB

Lord of Glory, I stand in agreement with Your eternal commission
that all nations must hear the Gospel and be discipled. I lift up my
pastor and ministers around the world, declaring that they are
graced with heavenly authority to go, baptize, and teach with divine
wisdom and power. Let their labor not be in vain but fruitful in
making disciples who walk in obedience to Your Word.

Father, I decree that every time my pastor preaches or teaches,
disciples are being formed—mature, steadfast, and rooted in
Christ. Raise up sons and daughters who will carry the Gospel to
their spheres of influence, multiplying the witness of Your Word in
schools, workplaces, and communities.

I intercede for the nations, O Lord. Open doors for ministers of the
Gospel to step into unreached territories. Protect them with Your
presence, just as You promised to be with them always. Let signs
and wonders confirm their message, making the teaching of Your
commands undeniable and irresistible.

Empower the global Church to embrace this commission with urgency. Let no nation, tribe, or tongue remain untouched. Baptize multitudes into the fellowship of the Father, Son, and Holy Spirit, sealing them with eternal life.

I decree that the end-time harvest shall be massive and glorious. As my pastor and Your servants obey the call, let revival sweep across nations until the knowledge of the Lord covers the earth as the waters cover the sea.

In Jesus' name, Amen.

WEEK 2: BOLDNESS AND GROWTH AMID PERSECUTION

The Gospel is never advanced in silence—it is proclaimed in power, often in the very face of resistance. Throughout history, the Word of God has spread most rapidly not in times of ease, but in times of persecution. When the enemy attempts to silence the Church, the Spirit fills believers with fresh boldness. Where trials press in, the Word breaks forth with greater force.

This week, our prayers rise for courage, resilience, and fearless proclamation of God's Word. The Scriptures show us that suffering does not weaken the Gospel—it strengthens its witness. The apostles counted it joy to suffer for Christ, and their testimony ignited revival. Chains could not bind the Word; threats could not silence it; even death could not quench its fire. Instead, the Gospel multiplied, and the name of Jesus spread to new territories.

We will intercede for pastors and ministers facing hostility, asking God to clothe them with unwavering boldness. We will declare that trials shall not intimidate the Church but will instead serve as a stage for God's glory. We will pray for believers in nations where persecution is fierce, asking the Lord to sustain them, embolden them, and cause their witness to shine like light in the darkest places.

This theme calls us to embrace a Kingdom paradox: that opposition often fuels expansion. As we lift up God's servants in prayer, we declare that no prison, no threat, and no weapon of man can halt the progress of His Word. The blood of the martyrs has always been seed for revival, and the courage of today's saints will continue to spark movements of the Spirit. This week, we align our intercession with the unstoppable advance of the Word—even amid persecution.

DAY 8

FEARLESS IN OPPOSITION

"But having suffered before and been shamefully treated,
as you know, at Philippi, we grew bold in our God to tell
you the Good News of God in much conflict."
—1 Thessalonians 2:2 WEB

Mighty God, Captain of our salvation, I lift up my voice today in prophetic declaration over my pastor and over every minister of the Gospel around the world: they shall not shrink back in fear, but they shall be bold as lions. Even when shame, rejection, or conflict arise, I decree by Your Spirit that holy boldness fills their tongues and a fiery conviction grips their hearts to preach the Good News without compromise.

Lord, I intercede that every place where opposition arises will become a fertile ground for Your Word to take root and flourish. Let every shameful treatment, every slander, every prison, and every storm be turned into a pulpit of glory where Your Gospel resounds louder than before. I declare that my pastor will not be silenced by intimidation, but rather strengthened by Your Spirit to declare truth with authority and clarity.

Father, clothe them with courage that does not bend under pressure, with faith that does not waver in adversity, and with joy that cannot be stolen by persecution. Surround their family with divine covering and let no arrow of the enemy prevail against their household.

I call forth supernatural growth in the midst of opposition. Let the harder the ground, the deeper the roots of the Word go forth. Let resistance birth revival, and let persecution push the message of Christ into new territories with unstoppable force.

In this season, I proclaim that their voice will echo with the sound of heaven and multitudes will turn to righteousness. What the enemy meant for harm, Lord, turn into platforms of divine testimony. Let Your Church rise fearless, bold, and triumphant.

In Jesus' name, Amen.

DAY 9

CHAINS FOR THE GOSPEL'S ADVANCE

"Now I desire to have you know, brothers, that the things which happened to me have turned out rather to the progress of the Good News; so that it became evident to the whole palace guard, and to all the rest, that I am in chains for Christ; and most of the brothers in the Lord, being confident through my bonds, are more abundantly bold to speak the word of God without fear."
—Philippians 1:12-14 WEB

Father of Glory, Sovereign Lord, I decree today that every setback experienced by Your servants will be transformed into setups for the advance of the Gospel. I intercede for my pastor and for all ministers laboring under pressure: let their trials and chains become testimonies that awaken boldness in the Church. What the enemy intends to silence, Lord, You will amplify.

I proclaim that the fire of courage will spread through the Body of Christ as ministers endure hardship with steadfast faith. Lord, may my pastor's steadfastness in difficulty inspire believers to rise in fearless proclamation. Let prison walls, hospital rooms, courtrooms, or public ridicule become pulpits where the testimony of Jesus shines brighter.

Holy Spirit, breathe upon the Church a new confidence. Cause men and women to see beyond their suffering into the eternal weight of glory being produced. Let courage rise among the saints as they witness endurance in their leaders. Release divine favor in every system—palaces, governments, media, and institutions—that the Good News may resound even in hostile environments.

Lord, let fearlessness seize the hearts of young and old alike. I decree that the more persecution increases, the greater the boldness will surge in the Church. My pastor shall stand, not broken by adversity, but burning with passion that infects others with holy zeal.

May the nations testify: "These are men and women chained for Christ, yet their message runs free." Let nothing bind the Word, O God.

In Jesus' name, Amen.

DAY 10

THE WORD IS NOT BOUND

"Remember Jesus Christ, risen from the dead, of the offspring of David, according to my Good News, in which I suffer hardship to the point of chains as a criminal. But God's word isn't chained."
—2 Timothy 2:8-9 WEB

Almighty God, Everlasting King, I proclaim today that Your Word cannot be bound. I intercede with fervency for my pastor and for ministers worldwide who carry the Gospel amid hardships. Let them never forget that though they may suffer in body or reputation, the message they carry is indestructible and unstoppable.

Father, I decree supernatural resilience over their minds and hearts. When the enemy seeks to wear them down with accusations, betrayals, or restrictions, lift their eyes to the risen Christ who conquered death and triumphed over every power. Let the memory of the empty tomb fuel their courage to press forward regardless of earthly chains.

I ask You, Lord, to send angelic reinforcement to sustain their assignments. Cause the proclamation of the Word to multiply, even in the most restricted regions. Let underground churches flourish, let hidden gatherings overflow, and let ministers find strength to speak even if it costs them their freedom.

Lord, I cover my pastor in the power of endurance. May they see hardship not as defeat but as a testimony that the Word is advancing beyond walls and barriers. Let Your Spirit lift their voice in places they cannot physically go, and let their message travel where they are denied access.

I decree that persecution will never imprison the Word. Let every chain fall in the Spirit, every prison become a place of evangelism, and every opposition turn into a stage for Christ's victory.

In Jesus' name, Amen.

DAY 11

SCATTERED BUT UNSTOPPABLE

"Saul was consenting to his death. A great persecution arose against the assembly which was in Jerusalem in that day. They were all scattered abroad throughout the regions of Judea and Samaria, except for the apostles. Devout men buried Stephen and lamented greatly over him. But Saul ravaged the assembly, entering into every house and dragging both men and women off to prison. Therefore those who were scattered abroad went around preaching the word."
—Acts 8:1-4 WEB

Lord of Hosts, I lift up my voice with urgency today, declaring that no scattering of Your servants shall silence their witness. I intercede for my pastor and every Gospel laborer who faces harassment, rejection, or dispersion: let every forced movement become a divine mission. What the enemy sought to crush, let it multiply across nations.

I decree that persecution will only extend the reach of the Gospel. Just as fire spreads when the wind blows, so let Your Word spread when opposition rises. Father, let every scattering of Your people ignite fresh flames of evangelism in homes, streets, cities, and nations.

Cover my pastor with boldness that refuses to be silenced. Even when pressured, let their voice ring stronger. Let grief be turned into greater resolve, and let opposition fuel deeper devotion. I ask

You, Lord, to take every weapon formed against them and convert it into a tool for kingdom expansion.

Father, may the testimony of those who endure persecution inspire believers across the earth to step out of comfort zones and preach with holy urgency. Let households, workplaces, and communities become platforms for the Gospel as believers carry the Word wherever they go.

I prophesy that what begins as scattering will end as revival. Nations shall hear the message of Christ because of faithful witnesses who refuse to bow under pressure. The Word shall not retreat—it will run and be glorified.

In Jesus' name, Amen.

DAY 12

UNASHAMED OF THE GOSPEL

"For I am not ashamed of the Good News of Christ,
because it is the power of God for salvation for everyone
who believes; for the Jew first, and also for the Greek."
—Romans 1:16 WEB

Righteous Father, I proclaim with boldness today: the Gospel of Christ is the power of God unto salvation! I intercede for my pastor and every minister that they shall carry this conviction without shame, hesitation, or fear. Let their preaching be infused with the raw power of Your Spirit to save, heal, and deliver all who believe.

Lord, let the fire of holy boldness burn in their hearts. Strip away timidity, doubt, or fear of rejection. May they stand unashamed before crowds great and small, before cultures hostile and receptive, declaring that Jesus is the only way. Let their confidence be rooted not in human wisdom but in the eternal power of the cross and resurrection.

I decree over them supernatural doors of opportunity to proclaim the Good News in places where it has been silenced. Open platforms in media, government, education, and the marketplace. Let them carry this message with dignity and authority, igniting faith in every hearer.

Father, I plead that the power of the Gospel will back every word they preach with signs following. Let miracles, deliverances, and transformed lives testify that the Good News is alive and active.

May entire families, communities, and nations encounter salvation through their unashamed witness.

I prophesy that no cultural opposition, intellectual argument, or demonic resistance will suppress the Word. Instead, the Gospel will thunder across the earth, shaking hearts and drawing multitudes into the Kingdom.

In Jesus' name, Amen.

DAY 13

TREASURE IN EARTHEN VESSELS

"But we have this treasure in clay vessels, that the exceeding greatness of the power may be of God, and not from ourselves. We are pressed on every side, yet not crushed; perplexed, yet not to despair; pursued, yet not forsaken; struck down, yet not destroyed; always carrying in the body the putting to death of the Lord Jesus, that the life of Jesus may also be revealed in our body. For we who live are always delivered to death for Jesus' sake, that the life also of Jesus may be revealed in our mortal flesh. So then death works in us, but life in you."
—2 Corinthians 4:7-12 WEB

Holy and Exalted One, I declare today that though Your servants are but earthen vessels, the treasure within them is indestructible. I intercede for my pastor and ministers across the nations: though pressed, they shall not be crushed; though struck down, they shall not be destroyed. Let the surpassing greatness of Your power shine forth through their weakness.

Lord, strengthen their inner man with resilience that cannot be broken by trials. When confusion surrounds them, let Your wisdom guide their steps. When they are pursued by enemies, assure them of Your nearness. When they are struck by betrayal or loss, let resurrection life arise within them.

Father, I pray that their suffering will become a stage for the revelation of Jesus. Let every wound, every scar, and every hardship testify of Christ's death and resurrection. May their lives pour out like a living sacrifice that births life in others.

I decree that endurance shall clothe them, hope shall anchor them, and joy shall sustain them. Their ministries shall not collapse under pressure but will shine brighter in adversity, revealing Christ to those they serve.

Let the life of Jesus be made manifest in their preaching, in their prayer, and in their daily walk. Lord, let the treasure within them draw nations into the light of the Gospel.

In Jesus' name, Amen.

DAY 14

PRAYER FOR UNITY AND BOLDNESS

"Not for these only do I pray, but for those also who
believe in me through their word, that they may all be one;
even as you, Father, are in me, and I in you, that they also
may be one in us; that the world may believe that you sent
me."
—John 17:20-21 WEB

Eternal Father, I declare in alignment with Christ's own
intercession: let the Church be one, even as You are One with the
Son. I lift my pastor and all ministers of the Word across the globe
before You—knit them together in holy unity, that their boldness
may be amplified and their witness made undeniable.

Lord, I ask that You strip away division, jealousy, and competition.
Instead, crown them with humility and bind their hearts with cords
of love. Let their unity be a prophetic testimony to the world that
Christ has indeed come. I decree that when they stand as one, their
preaching will thunder with multiplied power and their message
will pierce nations.

Father, strengthen my pastor with the boldness that flows from
knowing they are not alone. Surround them with covenant
relationships, prayer shields, and fellow laborers who share the
same passion for Your Kingdom. Where ministers feel isolated,
connect them divinely with like-minded warriors.

I prophesy that this unity will dismantle the strategies of the enemy. Where persecution rises, the Church will not scatter in fear but will rally together in love, advancing the Gospel with unstoppable force. Lord, let oneness be their fortress and love be their weapon.

Through their unity and fearless proclamation, let the world know Jesus Christ is Lord and that He was sent by You to redeem mankind. Let this oneness draw in harvests of souls and glorify Your Name across the earth.

In Jesus' name, Amen.

WEEK 3: BY SIGNS AND WONDERS, CONFIRMING THE WORD

The Gospel is not mere words on a page; it is power unleashed by the Spirit of God. Wherever the Word is preached, heaven longs to confirm it with signs, wonders, and undeniable demonstrations of divine authority. Miracles are not distractions from the message—they are confirmations of it, evidence that the risen Christ is still working among His people.

This week, our prayers focus on supernatural confirmation of the Word. We are reminded that when the apostles declared Christ boldly, healings broke forth, demons fled, and entire cities turned to the Lord. The power of God validated their testimony and silenced the opposition of skeptics. Today, that same power is available to every believer, and the same Spirit longs to reveal Christ with signs following.

We will intercede for pastors, evangelists, and Gospel ministers, asking the Lord to stretch forth His hand through them with healing and deliverance. We will pray for an increase in prophetic utterance, miracles of provision, and works of power that glorify Jesus and draw souls to repentance. Our focus is not on spectacle, but on transformation—lives changed, bodies healed, and nations awakened to the reality of God.

In a world saturated with arguments, philosophies, and competing voices, signs and wonders remain a heavenly signature that the Word being proclaimed is true. We believe that the Spirit still confirms His Word, and that miracles are part of the inheritance of the Church. As we engage in prophetic intercession this week, we call for fresh demonstrations of God's power to break forth, so that the Gospel is not only heard but seen in undeniable impact. By signs and wonders, the Word will be confirmed, and Christ will be exalted.

DAY 15

BOLDNESS AND HEAVENLY POWER

"When they heard it, they lifted up their voice to God with one accord, and said, 'O Lord, you are God, who made the heaven, the earth, the sea, and all that is in them; who by the mouth of your servant David said, "Why do the nations rage, and the peoples plot a vain thing? The kings of the earth take a stand, and the rulers take council together, against the Lord, and against his Christ." For truly, in this city against your holy servant, Jesus, whom you anointed, both Herod and Pontius Pilate, with the Gentiles and the people of Israel, were gathered together to do whatever your hand and your council foreordained to happen. Now, Lord, look at their threats, and grant to your servants to speak your word with all boldness, while you stretch out your hand to heal; and that signs and wonders may be done through the name of your holy Servant Jesus.' When they had prayed, the place was shaken where they were gathered together. They were all filled with the Holy Spirit, and they spoke the word of God with boldness."

— Acts 4:24-31 WEB

Sovereign Lord, Creator of heaven and earth, I lift my voice in unison with the saints who have gone before me, declaring Your greatness and Your rule over every nation, every ruler, and every power. I exalt You as the God whose counsel cannot be overturned, whose Word runs swiftly and prevails, and whose Christ has triumphed over death, hell, and the grave.

Today I stand in the gap for my pastor and every minister of the Gospel, declaring that the same Spirit who filled the early Church fills them with holy boldness. No intimidation, no threat, no opposition shall silence their proclamation of truth. Let courage rise like fire within their bones, and let their lips never falter in declaring the unshakable message of Christ.

Stretch forth Your mighty hand, O God, to heal the sick, raise the oppressed, and set captives free through the preaching of Your Word. Let undeniable signs and wonders confirm the testimony of Christ, so that multitudes will turn from idols to the living God. Cause every gathering where Your Word is proclaimed to be shaken with heavenly power and filled with the glory of Your Spirit.

Father, I call for an outpouring of miracles in my pastor's ministry and in the global Church. Let churches become furnaces of divine fire, where healings, deliverances, and prophetic demonstrations bear witness to the living Christ. Transform cities and nations as the Word is carried forth, not in persuasive speech alone, but in the demonstration of the Spirit and of power.

Lord, crown Your servants with divine authority, that everywhere they go, demons tremble, chains break, and Your Word spreads like wildfire. May their labor be marked with fruit that remains and testimonies that magnify the name of Jesus.

In Jesus' name, Amen.

DAY 16

SPEAKING BOLDLY IN GRACE

"Therefore they stayed there a long time, speaking boldly
in the Lord, who testified to the word of his grace, granting
signs and wonders to be done by their hands."
— Acts 14:3 WEB

Mighty Father, I declare today that You are the God who confirms
the word of Your grace with power. Your Gospel is not in word only,
but in power, in the Holy Spirit, and in much assurance. I call upon
Your covenant faithfulness to strengthen my pastor and ministers
around the world with an enduring boldness to speak in the Lord
without fear or retreat.

I decree that as they stand before congregations, crowds, or
individuals, Your Spirit will bear witness to their words, saturating
them with grace and heavenly authority. Let no environment be too
hostile, no opposition too strong, for You are the One who grants
boldness beyond human strength.

Father, release signs and wonders through their hands. Let miracles
erupt like streams in the desert, confirming to every skeptic that
Your Word is alive. Open blind eyes, heal broken bodies, restore
shattered minds, and raise the dead as testimony to the Gospel of
Christ. Cause every act of power to magnify Jesus, never man, so
that nations may know that salvation belongs to the Lord.

I lift before You ministers who are weary or under attack, asking
that You clothe them with new strength and mantle them with fresh

grace. Renew their vision, refresh their faith, and surround them with angelic reinforcement as they contend for souls in this hour.

Lord, may the word of Your grace not be hindered but flow freely through pulpits, altars, homes, and streets. Let testimonies multiply and cities be shaken with the reality of Your kingdom.

In Jesus' name, Amen.

DAY 17

TRIUMPH OVER FALSE POWERS

"But some of the Jewish exorcists, who went from place to place, attempted to invoke over those who had the evil spirits the name of the Lord Jesus, saying, 'We adjure you by Jesus whom Paul preaches.' There were seven sons of one Sceva, a Jewish chief priest, who did this. The evil spirit answered, 'Jesus I know, and Paul I know, but who are you?' The man in whom the evil spirit was leaped on them, mastered them all, and prevailed against them, so that they fled out of that house naked and wounded. This became known to all, both Jews and Greeks, who lived at Ephesus. Fear fell on them all, and the name of the Lord Jesus was magnified. Many also of those who had believed came, confessing, and declaring their deeds. Many of those who practiced magical arts brought their books together and burned them in the sight of all. They counted their price, and found it to be fifty thousand pieces of silver. So the word of the Lord was growing and becoming mighty."
— Acts 19:13-20 WEB

Almighty God, I lift high the name of Jesus—the Name above all names, before which every knee must bow and every demon must tremble. I declare that the authority of Christ rests upon my pastor and ministers across the earth, and they are known in the spirit realm as carriers of divine power.

Lord, let no counterfeit, no sorcery, no false anointing prevail against the truth of the Gospel. Cause every spirit of deception, witchcraft, and occult practice to bow before the name of Jesus as Your servants proclaim the Word. May their ministries be marked by undeniable demonstrations of kingdom authority that strip darkness of its influence and magnify Christ.

I decree that the Word in their mouths shall dismantle principalities and powers, leading to public renunciations of sin and falsehood. Let chains of addiction, idolatry, and immorality be broken as people confess and forsake their works of darkness. May entire communities witness transformation, as in Ephesus, where many repented and cast away idols.

Father, let the fear of the Lord fall upon multitudes again. Let awe and reverence grip cities, stirring repentance and holy reverence for Your Son. May the Word of the Lord grow mightily and prevail, silencing every voice of the enemy.

Lord, establish my pastor as a vessel of uncompromising truth and unshakable power. May their ministry bear fruit that cannot be denied, and may the global Church arise in purity, holiness, and power, advancing the kingdom with unstoppable force.

In Jesus' name, Amen.

DAY 18

SIGNS FOLLOWING THE PREACHED WORD

"These signs will accompany those who believe: in my name they will cast out demons; they will speak with new languages; they will take up serpents; and if they drink any deadly thing, it will in no way hurt them; they will lay hands on the sick, and they will recover." ... "They went out and preached everywhere, the Lord working with them, and confirming the word by the signs that followed. Amen."
— Mark 16:17-20 WEB

Lord of glory, I declare that the Gospel is never powerless, for You have ordained that signs will follow those who believe. Today I stand as an intercessor for my pastor and for ministers across the globe, calling forth the manifestation of Your Word in signs, wonders, and mighty works.

Father, let the authority of the name of Jesus be magnified in their ministries. As they lay hands on the sick, let bodies be healed. As they confront demonic powers, let strongholds collapse and captives be set free. Let the reality of Your kingdom be seen not in words only, but in undeniable demonstrations of divine authority.

I decree protection over them as they labor in dangerous fields, where serpents and deadly forces abound. No weapon formed against them shall prosper. The power of the blood of Jesus covers them, shielding them from every scheme of the enemy.

Lord, I call for fresh fire to rest upon them as they go forth. Let every message they preach be confirmed with visible signs of Your hand at work. May miracles break forth not as isolated events but as continual streams that testify that Jesus Christ is alive.

Let the global Church walk in the fullness of this promise—that signs will follow all who believe. Empower believers everywhere to heal the sick, deliver the oppressed, and proclaim salvation with supernatural backing.

In Jesus' name, Amen.

DAY 19

AUTHORITY OVER SERPENTS AND DARKNESS

"Behold, I give you authority to tread on serpents and scorpions, and over all the power of the enemy. Nothing will in any way hurt you. Nevertheless, don't rejoice in this, that the spirits are subject to you, but rejoice that your names are written in heaven."
— Luke 10:19-20 WEB

Majestic King, I exalt You as the One who has granted authority to Your servants over all the power of the enemy. You have given us the right to trample serpents, scorpions, and every manifestation of darkness, and I decree that my pastor and ministers of the Gospel walk in this kingdom mandate with unshakable confidence.

I lift them before You, asking that they never shrink back from confronting demonic powers but move forward clothed in the authority of Christ. Let every foul spirit be subject to the name of Jesus in their mouths. May chains of oppression, sickness, and torment fall swiftly at the command of Your Word through their lips.

Yet, Lord, I pray they remain anchored in humility, rejoicing not merely in demonstrations of power but in the eternal reality that their names are written in heaven. Keep their hearts tender, their spirits aligned with Yours, and their motives pure.

I decree divine protection over their lives, families, and ministries. No harm shall overtake them; no scheme of the enemy shall prevail. As they tread upon the works of darkness, let them do so with joy, peace, and assurance of eternal victory.

Father, let this same authority saturate the global Church. Raise up a fearless generation of ministers who operate with wisdom, boldness, and love, making Christ known in power and in truth.

In Jesus' name, Amen.

DAY 20

GOD ALSO BEARING WITNESS

"How will we escape if we neglect so great a salvation?—
which at the first having been spoken through the Lord,
was confirmed to us by those who heard; God also
testifying with them, both by signs and wonders, by
various works of power, and by gifts of the Holy Spirit,
according to his own will?"
— Hebrews 2:3-4 WEB

Faithful Father, I declare that You are the God who bears witness to the Gospel with signs and wonders. The message of salvation is no ordinary word but the living power of God unto salvation. Today I intercede for my pastor and for every minister who carries this word, asking that their proclamation be sealed with Your own testimony.

Lord, let not their words fall to the ground empty. Stretch forth Your hand in power, confirming their preaching with works that only You can perform. May healings, deliverances, prophetic utterances, and supernatural gifts flow unhindered, demonstrating that the Spirit of the Lord is upon them.

I decree that the gifts of the Spirit will operate in full measure in their lives—words of wisdom, knowledge, faith, healings, miracles, and discerning of spirits—distributed by Your will, to strengthen the Church and draw the lost to Christ.

Let the proclamation of salvation thunder across the nations, accompanied by wonders that silence the doubters and compel sinners to repentance. Cause the Word to spread like fire, advancing from house to house, city to city, and nation to nation, until Christ is exalted everywhere.

Father, strengthen my pastor with fresh grace. Anoint them as a vessel of purity and power, walking humbly before You while wielding heaven's authority. Let their ministry resound as a witness not of human might but of the living God.

In Jesus' name, Amen.

DAY 21

THE GOD OF SIGNS

"Moses answered, 'But, behold, they will not believe me, nor listen to my voice; for they will say, "The Lord has not appeared to you."' The Lord said to him, 'What is that in your hand?' He said, 'A rod.' He said, 'Throw it on the ground.' He threw it on the ground, and it became a snake; and Moses ran away from it. The Lord said to Moses, 'Stretch out your hand, and take it by the tail.' He stretched out his hand, and laid hold of it, and it became a rod in his hand. 'This is so that they may believe that the Lord, the God of their fathers, the God of Abraham, the God of Isaac, and the God of Jacob, has appeared to you.'"
— Exodus 4:1-9 WEB

Eternal God, the One who calls and equips, I exalt You as the God of signs and wonders. You reveal Yourself through power that cannot be denied, and You grant assurance to Your servants that You have indeed sent them. I stand in the gap for my pastor and for ministers everywhere, decreeing that the works of their hands will testify that You have called and anointed them.

Lord, where doubt or resistance rises against their voice, confirm their message with signs that none can refute. Let the authority of heaven validate their words, proving that they are sent ones, carriers of divine commission. Cause miracles to erupt even from the simplest acts of obedience, that people may believe in the God of Abraham, Isaac, and Jacob.

I declare that the rod in their hand—their God-given assignment and authority—will become a sign to this generation. Whether through preaching, prayer, or acts of service, let every act release demonstrations of Your kingdom. Let spiritual serpents be subdued, and let the people know that the Lord has appeared to His servants.

Father, establish them as undeniable witnesses of Your glory. Let their ministries silence the lies of the enemy, awaken faith in the hearers, and compel multitudes to acknowledge Christ as Lord. May the global Church walk in this same mantle of demonstration, proving to every generation that our God is alive and mighty to save.

In Jesus' name, Amen.

WEEK 4: OVERCOMING OPPOSITION THROUGH SPIRITUAL WARFARE

The advancement of God's Word is not unchallenged—it is contested by powers of darkness that seek to silence truth and hinder the Gospel. Yet every opposition is an opportunity for the Church to wield her spiritual authority in Christ. The battlefield is real, but so is the victory already secured through the cross and resurrection of Jesus.

This week, we step into the posture of intercessors and warriors, contending for the protection of God's servants and the unstoppable progress of His Word. The Scriptures remind us that our warfare is not against flesh and blood but against principalities, powers, and spiritual wickedness. Resistance is not natural—it is spiritual. And therefore, the weapons we use are not carnal but mighty through God.

Our prayers will focus on tearing down strongholds that oppose the Word, shielding pastors and ministers from spiritual attacks, and declaring triumph over every adversary. We will intercede for angelic assistance, divine protection, and breakthrough against regional powers that resist the Gospel. We will plead the Blood of Jesus over ministries, declaring that the enemy cannot touch what belongs to God.

Through spiritual warfare, we partner with heaven's army to ensure that the Word continues to run swiftly and be glorified. As we pray, we affirm that no scheme of darkness, no intimidation, and no weapon formed against the Church will prevail. The enemy may rage, but he is already defeated. The saints overcome by the Blood of the Lamb and by the word of their testimony.

This week, our intercession rises as a battle cry, ensuring that the advance of God's Word is unstoppable, unbreakable, and victorious. Through warfare, we see triumph; through opposition, we see breakthrough; and through prayer, we see the Kingdom advance.

DAY 22

AN OPEN DOOR AMID ADVERSARIES

For a great and effective door is opened to me, and there are many adversaries.
—1 Corinthians 16:9 WEB

Almighty God, Commander of Heaven's armies, I lift my voice with holy fire to declare that no adversary can shut what You have opened. You are the Keeper of the keys, the One who sets before Your servants doors of divine opportunity that no man, no devil, no principality can close. I stand as an intercessor for my pastor and for every minister of the Gospel, declaring that the Word they preach shall not be hindered, but shall run swiftly and be glorified.

Father, I decree that every opposition, every subtle scheme of darkness, every spirit of intimidation rising against them be rendered powerless in the name of Jesus. I plead the Blood of the Lamb over their ministry, their household, and their assignments, erecting a hedge of divine protection that cannot be penetrated. Where adversaries gather to plot confusion and resistance, let them stumble and fall, for You are their Light and Salvation.

Lord, I pray that boldness be multiplied in their spirits, that their tongues may proclaim truth with fire, unafraid of ridicule or persecution. Anoint their eyes to see the strategies of the enemy before they manifest, and strengthen their hands to war and their fingers to battle. Let Your Word pierce through every resistance like a two-edged sword, dismantling arguments, demolishing pride, and planting seeds of eternal life in the hearts of hearers.

I declare that the open door You have set before them shall bear much fruit. The harvest shall not be delayed, and adversaries shall only serve as stepping stones for the greater display of Your glory. The Gospel shall advance, and Christ shall be magnified in all nations.

In Jesus' name, Amen.

DAY 23

Chains Broken by Prayer

Now about that time, Herod the king stretched out his
hands to oppress some of the assembly.

Peter therefore was kept in the prison, but constant prayer
was made by the assembly to God for him.

When they were past the first and the second guard, they
came to the iron gate that leads into the city, which opened
to them by itself, and they went out, and went down one
street, and immediately the angel departed from him.

On an appointed day, Herod dressed himself in royal
clothing, sat on the throne, and gave a speech to them. The
people shouted, "The voice of a god, and not of a man!"
Immediately an angel of the Lord struck him, because he
didn't give God the glory, then he was eaten by worms and
died.

But the word of God grew and multiplied.

—Acts 12:1, 5, 10, 21-24 WEB

Sovereign Deliverer, I arise in fervent intercession, calling forth
Your mighty intervention over pastors and ministers of the Gospel.
Just as You sent Your angel to release Peter from prison, so do I
decree supernatural deliverance for every servant bound by
spiritual or natural chains. Every iron gate of opposition, every
guard of wickedness stationed to restrict their movement, let it
swing open by divine power, granting them unhindered access to
fulfill Your mandate.

Father, where rulers and systems rise like Herod to oppress and silence the voice of truth, let Your judgment swiftly dismantle their pride. May no glory be stolen from You, the Lord of Hosts, but may every outcome testify that You alone are God. Expose the arrogance of oppressors, overthrow their schemes, and exalt the name of Jesus above every throne of man.

Lord, I pray for prevailing intercession in the body of Christ. Stir hearts to pray with constancy, with tears and travail, until breakthrough is manifested for Your servants. Let angelic intervention be released on their behalf—angels of deliverance, angels of protection, angels of provision—so that no power of darkness prevails against them.

I decree that every attempt to silence the Word shall fail. Instead, like in the days of the apostles, let the Word of God multiply and spread across cities, nations, and continents. Out of persecution, let revival flames burst forth. Out of opposition, let testimonies of deliverance resound.

In Jesus' name, Amen.

DAY 24

STRENGTHENED IN THE ARMOR OF GOD

Finally, be strong in the Lord, and in the strength of his might. Put on the whole armor of God, that you may be able to stand against the wiles of the devil. For our wrestling is not against flesh and blood, but against the principalities, against the powers, against the world's rulers of the darkness of this age, and against the spiritual forces of wickedness in the heavenly places. Therefore, put on the whole armor of God, that you may be able to withstand in the evil day, and having done all, to stand. Stand therefore, having the utility belt of truth buckled around your waist, and having put on the breastplate of righteousness, and having fitted your feet with the preparation of the Good News of peace, above all, taking up the shield of faith, with which you will be able to quench all the fiery darts of the evil one. Take the helmet of salvation, and the sword of the Spirit, which is the word of God; with all prayer and requests, praying at all times in the Spirit, and being watchful to this end in all perseverance and requests for all the saints.

—Ephesians 6:10-18 WEB

Lord of Glory, Mighty Warrior who trains our hands for battle, I lift up pastors and ministers who daily face the fury of spiritual adversaries. I proclaim that their strength is not in the flesh but in the unshakable might of the Lord of Hosts. I decree that they shall stand firm, clothed in the full armor of God, immovable in the evil day, and radiant with Your victory.

Father, gird their loins with truth so that lies and deception cannot sway them. Let the breastplate of righteousness guard their hearts against compromise and guilt. May their feet march swiftly in the Gospel of peace, unshaken by storms of strife or discord. Clothe their minds with the helmet of salvation, shielding them from confusion, despair, and fear.

Lord, I lift up the shield of faith on their behalf, extinguishing every fiery dart of slander, betrayal, doubt, and temptation. May their faith grow stronger in battle, proving Your faithfulness time and again. Place in their hands the sword of the Spirit, sharper than any weapon of darkness, empowering them to cut down strongholds and pierce through spiritual resistance with the living Word.

Holy Spirit, ignite them in constant prayer, stirring within them a relentless cry that never ceases. Let intercession rise for them across the earth, covering them in every nation, in every mission, in every pulpit. May they be watchful, vigilant, and victorious, conquering through Christ Jesus, until the kingdoms of this world bow before the King of kings.

In Jesus' name, Amen.

DAY 25

MIGHTY THROUGH GOD

For though we walk in the flesh, we don't wage war according to the flesh; for the weapons of our warfare are not of the flesh, but mighty before God to the throwing down of strongholds, throwing down imaginations and every high thing that is exalted against the knowledge of God, and bringing every thought into captivity to the obedience of Christ, and being in readiness to avenge all disobedience, when your obedience is made full.

—2 Corinthians 10:3-6 WEB

Captain of Salvation, I rise in Your authority to decree that my pastor and every minister of the Gospel shall not war in their own strength, but in the power of Your Spirit. They may walk in the flesh, but their battles are won in the realm of the Spirit, where Your weapons are mighty to demolish strongholds.

Father, I declare that every high tower of pride, false philosophy, deception, and rebellion raised against the knowledge of Christ be torn down by the power of Your Word. Let arguments collapse, let imaginations be shattered, and let every thought be brought under submission to the Lordship of Jesus Christ. May the pulpit they stand upon be an altar of truth that pulls down darkness and exalts Christ alone.

Lord, I pray that Your servants be filled with precision in the Spirit, wielding prayer, fasting, the Word, and prophetic declaration as weapons that never fail. I decree that witchcraft, sorcery, and every evil council raised against them shall be scattered in confusion. No scheme of hell shall prosper, and no curse shall alight upon them, for the weapons formed against them are nullified by the Blood of Jesus.

Father, as they remain obedient to Your call, let their obedience release vengeance against disobedience in the spirit realm. May their faithfulness strike terror in the camp of the enemy, and may nations bow as the knowledge of Christ spreads like fire. The Word shall advance, unhindered and unchained, for Your weapons are mighty and Your victory is eternal.

In Jesus' name, Amen.

DAY 26

RESISTING THE ENEMY

Be subject therefore to God. Resist the devil, and he will
flee from you. Draw near to God, and he will draw near to
you. Cleanse your hands, you sinners, and purify your
hearts, you double-minded.
—James 4:7-8 WEB

Holy Father, I cry out for my pastor and for ministers of the Gospel
everywhere, declaring that they are fully surrendered to You. Their
lives, ministries, and callings are submitted under Your mighty
hand, and therefore, they are empowered to resist the devil with
unshakable authority. I decree that every demonic pursuit against
them must flee in terror at the presence of Christ in them.

Lord, I pray for a deep drawing near. Let their altars of prayer burn
with ceaseless fire. May intimacy with You be their refuge, their
shield, and their source of unbreakable strength. As they come near,
let heaven open over their lives; let divine wisdom, revelation, and
fresh anointing be released without measure.

I intercede for their purity of hands and hearts. Wash them
continually in the Blood of the Lamb. May no hidden stain of sin,
compromise, or distraction entangle their feet. Let their hearts
remain undivided, consumed with one pursuit — to glorify Jesus
and advance His Kingdom in power.

Father, I declare that as they resist the enemy, strongholds are
broken, territories are claimed, and victories are won for the cause

of Christ. No spirit of fear, no arrow of temptation, no whisper of deception shall prevail. They shall stand holy, bold, and victorious, for You dwell with them and in them.

In Jesus' name, Amen.

DAY 27

STRENGTHENED BY HEAVENLY VISITATION

Then he said to me, "Don't be afraid, Daniel; for from the first day that you set your heart to understand, and to humble yourself before your God, your words were heard: and I have come for your words' sake.

But the prince of the kingdom of Persia withstood me twenty-one days; but behold, Michael, one of the chief princes, came to help me, because I remained there with the kings of Persia.

Now I have come to make you understand what will happen to your people in the latter days; for the vision is yet for many days."

When he had spoken to me according to these words, I set my face toward the ground, and was mute.

Behold, one in the likeness of the sons of men touched my lips: then I opened my mouth, and spoke and said to him who stood before me, "My lord, by reason of the vision my sorrows are returned to me, and I retain no strength."

Then one like the appearance of a man touched me again, and he strengthened me.

He said, "Greatly beloved man, don't be afraid: peace be to you, be strong, yes, be strong." When he spoke to me, I was strengthened, and said, "Let my lord speak; for you have strengthened me."

—Daniel 10:12-19 WEB

Eternal King, who sends angelic hosts to war for the destiny of Your people, I lift my voice to declare divine intervention over pastors and ministers of the Gospel. Just as Daniel's prayers were heard from the first day, so do I decree that the intercessions and cries of Your servants shall not fall to the ground. Their petitions are received, and heavenly reinforcements are released on their behalf.

Father, I decree that every prince of Persia — every regional principality, every ruling spirit that resists the advancement of the Word — be subdued and overthrown by angelic forces sent from Your throne. Let Michael and the host of heaven fight on behalf of every minister, ensuring that their messages, assignments, and visions reach their fulfillment without delay.

Lord, when weariness overtakes them, touch them with Your hand of strength. Let the fire of Your presence restore their voices, renew their strength, and impart courage to stand and not faint. May they hear Your voice whispering, "Peace be to you, be strong, yes, be strong." Let divine encounters ignite their spirits, assuring them that heaven is backing their mission.

Father, I declare that supernatural understanding be released to them, granting clarity of vision for their generation. Let no fog of confusion or heaviness hinder their prophetic insight. May every word they release carry the authority of heaven, breaking through opposition and establishing Your will upon the earth.

In Jesus' name, Amen.

DAY 28

OVERCOMING BY THE BLOOD

They overcame him because of the Lamb's blood, and
because of the word of their testimony. They didn't love
their life, even to death.
—Revelation 12:11 WEB

Lion of Judah, I proclaim the triumph of the Blood of the Lamb over
my pastor and ministers across the nations. The Blood speaks better
things than any accusation of the enemy, silencing every voice of
condemnation, every curse, and every strategy of darkness. By the
Blood, I decree their victory is sealed, their authority is established,
and their lives are hidden in Christ.

Father, I intercede that their testimonies rise as fiery weapons
against the accuser. Let every breakthrough, every deliverance,
every miracle You perform in their ministries resound as
undeniable proof that Jesus is alive. May their testimonies ignite
faith in multitudes, overturning the lies of the enemy and ushering
countless souls into the Kingdom.

Lord, I pray for unwavering courage. May they not shrink back in
fear or cling to self-preservation but live fully yielded to Your will.
If called to sacrifice, may they embrace it with the boldness of those
who love not their lives unto death, knowing that eternal glory far
outweighs earthly trials.

I decree that through the Blood and their testimony, opposition
shall bow, adversaries shall scatter, and the Gospel shall advance

with unstoppable force. The accuser is cast down, the Church arises in triumph, and the Word multiplies to the ends of the earth.

In Jesus' name, Amen.

DAY 29

WIELDING THE HIGH PRAISES

> Let the saints rejoice in honor. Let them sing for joy on
> their beds. May the high praises of God be in their
> mouths, and a two-edged sword in their hand; To execute
> vengeance on the nations, and punishments on the
> peoples; To bind their kings with chains, and their nobles
> with fetters of iron; To execute on them the written
> judgment. All his saints have this honor. Praise Yah!
> — Psalm 149:5-9 WEB

Almighty God, Captain of the Hosts of Heaven, I lift my voice in prophetic praise and intercession. I exalt You for arming Your people with both worship and warfare. I decree that the praises rising from the lips of the saints will become a mighty weapon in the Spirit, breaking strongholds, dismantling opposition, and clearing the way for the unhindered advance of Your Word.

I stand in the gap for my pastor and for every faithful shepherd You have anointed. Let their tongues be like sharpened swords of truth, cutting through deception and darkness. As they labor to declare the counsel of God, may every adversary be silenced, and every plan of wickedness be overturned by the execution of Your written judgment. I proclaim that the chains of resistance are shattered by the high praises of Zion.

Father, I surround Your ministers across the nations with an atmosphere of worship that paralyzes the enemy. Let the sound of victory echo in their hearts even as they face trials. May they wield the two-edged sword of Your Word with precision, binding spiritual rulers and dethroning powers of darkness that rise against the Gospel.

By faith, I release songs of deliverance that become warfare in the spirit realm. Where oppression has tried to silence Your servants, let Your joy be their strength and their shield. Where intimidation has sought to break their resolve, let holy boldness and supernatural courage rise from within them.

I declare that every assignment of the adversary against the advancement of the Word is nullified. The glory of the Lord will be their rear guard, and the praises of His people will be their weapon. The Word will not be hindered, but will run swiftly and be glorified in every land.

In Jesus' name, Amen.

DAY 30

TREADING ON SERPENTS AND SCORPIONS

> Now after these things, the Lord also appointed seventy others, and sent them two by two ahead of him into every city and place, where he was about to come. Then he said to them, "The harvest is indeed plentiful, but the laborers are few. Pray therefore to the Lord of the harvest, that he may send out laborers into his harvest. Go your ways. Behold, I send you out as lambs among wolves… The seventy returned with joy, saying, "Lord, even the demons are subject to us in your name!" He said to them, "I saw Satan having fallen like lightning from heaven. Behold, I give you authority to tread on serpents and scorpions, and over all the power of the enemy. Nothing will in any way hurt you."
> — Luke 10:1-3, 17-19 WEB

Lord of the Harvest and Giver of Authority, I exalt You for commissioning laborers and equipping them with power over all the works of the enemy. Today I stand in intercession for my pastor, and for every messenger You have sent forth into the harvest fields of the earth. I proclaim that no wolf, no serpent, no scorpion, and no demonic adversary will be able to withstand the authority of Christ that rests upon them.

Father, I plead the covering of the Lamb's blood over those You have sent. As they enter hostile territories, let the fragrance of Christ overwhelm the stench of darkness. Cause every demonic assault against their minds, their health, their families, and their ministries to be scattered like chaff before the wind. Let their feet be swift with the Gospel, trampling upon every serpent-spirit of deception and every scorpion-sting of accusation.

I declare by faith that Satan has already fallen like lightning, and his power is broken. The ministers of God will not be intimidated nor wounded by the snares of the wicked. Their joy will overflow as testimonies of deliverance and salvation abound. Their lips will resound with reports of demons fleeing, of captives being freed, and of lives transformed by the unshakable power of Your Word.

Holy Spirit, clothe them with boldness and discernment. Let every word they speak carry the fire of Heaven and pierce the hearts of those bound in darkness. Multiply their strength, magnify their effectiveness, and grant them divine protection from all harm.

I proclaim that the Word of the Lord will run without obstruction in every city, every nation, and every generation. The laborers will not faint, the wolves will not prevail, and the victory of Christ will be manifest.

In Jesus' name, Amen.

DAY 31

EYES OPENED TO SEE VICTORY

> When the servant of the man of God had risen early, and
> gone out, behold, an army with horses and chariots was
> around the city. His servant said to him, "Alas, my master!
> What shall we do?" He answered, "Don't be afraid, for
> those who are with us are more than those who are with
> them." Elisha prayed, and said, "Yahweh, please open his
> eyes, that he may see." Yahweh opened the young man's
> eyes, and he saw; and behold, the mountain was full of
> horses and chariots of fire around Elisha.
>
> — 2 Kings 6:15-17 WEB

Sovereign Lord, Commander of Angel Armies, I lift up my heart in
confidence and prophetic decree. I exalt You as the God who
surrounds Your people with chariots of fire. I declare that my pastor
and every minister of the Gospel will never be outnumbered,
outflanked, or overcome, for greater are those with them than those
against them.

Father, I intercede for spiritual sight to be opened in the lives of
Your servants. Where fear has tried to blind them, unveil the
heavenly armies that stand at their side. Let them know that Your
protection is not fragile, but fierce; not invisible, but invincible. As
opposition gathers around their ministries, let them perceive the
fiery host that encamps about those who fear You.

I decree that the enemy's encirclement will be turned into a
testimony of deliverance. The snares laid against them will be

broken, and the armies of darkness will be scattered by the brightness of Your presence. Empower them to speak with authority, pray with fire, and minister with unshakable boldness, knowing that Heaven backs their every step.

Lord, strengthen their hearts against despair. When they face overwhelming resistance, remind them of the unseen victory already secured. May angelic reinforcements be dispatched to shield, to fight, and to advance the purposes of the Kingdom wherever they labor.

I proclaim that the global church will not cower before the threats of darkness. The Word of God will continue to spread, multiply, and prevail, carried forward by men and women whose eyes have been opened to see the host of Heaven at work.

In Jesus' name, Amen.

EPILOGUE

The prayers have been spoken, the Scriptures declared, and the intercession released—but the true work begins now. Prayer is not confined to the pages of a book. It is a call to a lifestyle, a daily surrender to stand in the gap for the Word of God to advance. The nations will not be changed by wishful thinking or half-hearted petitions, but by believers who embrace the labor of intercession as a holy mandate.

You have prayed for boldness, for protection, for provision, and for supernatural confirmation of the Word. Now the challenge is this: will you continue? Will you become the voice that consistently cries out until revival springs forth, until missionaries are sent, until pastors are strengthened, until the Word spreads in power across every border?

History is still being written, and heaven still listens for the sound of the saints. Your prayers matter. They tilt the balance in unseen battles, they strengthen weary servants, they prepare the soil for harvest. The kingdom of darkness trembles when even one believer commits to unceasing intercession.

So I leave you with this charge: do not let this be the end. Let it be the beginning of a deeper partnership with God's purposes. Keep praying until the Word runs freely. Keep interceding until the knowledge of the Lord covers the earth as the waters cover the sea.

And when you feel weak, remember this: the Spirit Himself intercedes through you with groanings too deep for words.

Stand firm. Pray boldly. And watch the Word of God advance through your prayers.

ENCOURAGE OTHERS WITH YOUR STORY

If this prayer guide has strengthened your faith, deepened your intercession, or helped you stand in the gap, would you consider leaving a short review on Amazon? Your feedback not only encourages others but also helps more believers discover this resource and join in the prayer movement. Every review—just a few sentences—makes a difference. Thank you for being part of this movement.

More from PrayerScripts

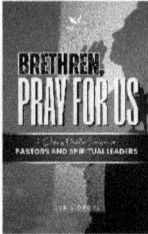

"Brethren, Pray For Us" Series

Brethren, Pray for Us:

31 Days of Prophetic Intercession for Pastors and Spiritual Leaders

They pray for us. But who prays for them?

Shepherds After My Heart:

31 Days of Prophetic Intercession for Raising Godly Shepherds and Flocks After God's Own Heart

Pastors, ministers, and spiritual leaders pour out daily to feed, guide, and protect the flock of God—but who stands in the gap for them?

Advancing the Word of God:

31 Days of Prophetic Intercession to See God's Word Multiply, Prevail, and Transform Lives

What if your prayers could push the Gospel forward, strengthen weary pastors, and open doors for God's Word to multiply across the nations?

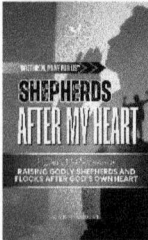

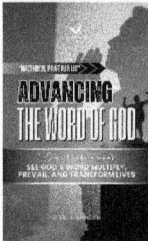

Command Your Morning:

30 Days of Prayers and Declarations to Seize Your Day and Shape Your Destiny

There is a battle over every morning—and every believer must choose to either drift into the day or command it.

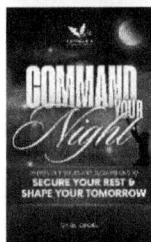

Command Your Night:

30 Days of Prayers and Declarations to Secure Your Rest and Shape Your Tomorrow

Every night is a spiritual battlefield—what you do before you sleep can determine the course of your tomorrow.

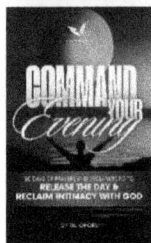

Command Your Evening:

30 Days of Prayers and Declarations to Release the Day and Reclaim Intimacy with God

There is a battle over every transition—and evening is one of the most spiritually neglected.

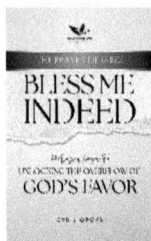

Bless Me Indeed:

Unlocking the Overflow of God's Favor

What if you could activate God's favor in your life today and walk in blessings that surpass your wildest expectations?

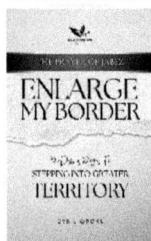

Enlarge My Border:

Stepping Into Greater Territory

Do you feel like you're living beneath your full potential? Do limitations, setbacks, and invisible barriers keep you from stepping into all God has promised? It's time to lift your cry for enlargement.

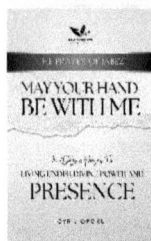

May Your Hand Be With Me:

Living Under Divine Power and Presence

What happens when the mighty hand of God rests upon your life? Doors open that no man can shut. Strength rises where weakness once prevailed. Guidance comes in the midst of confusion, and protection surrounds you in every battle.

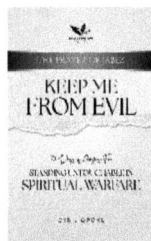

Keep Me From Evil:

Standing Untouchable in Spiritual Warfare

What if the enemy's plans could never touch you or your family? Imagine walking through life completely protected, untouchable, and victorious—no matter what schemes are formed against you.

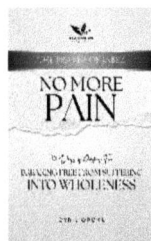

No More Pain:

Breaking Free from Suffering into Wholeness

Have you been carrying the weight of sorrow, disappointment, or hidden wounds for far too long? Do cycles of pain seem to repeat in your life, your marriage, or your family?

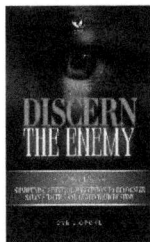

Discern the Enemy:

Sharpening Spiritual Perception to Recognize Satan's Tactics and Guard Your Destiny

The greatest danger is not the enemy you can see—it is the one you cannot. Can you recognize the enemy before he strikes?

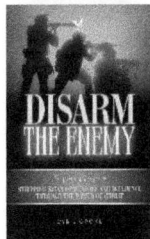

Disarm the Enemy:

Stripping Satan of Weapons and Influence Through the Power of Christ

Are you tired of feeling like the enemy has the upper hand in your life? It's time to take back your ground, silence the lies of darkness, and walk in the unstoppable authority of Christ.

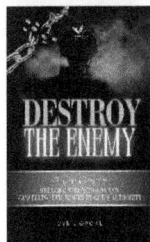

Destroy the Enemy:

Breaking Strongholds and Cancelling Evil Works by God's Authority

Are you tired of living under the weight of unseen battles? It's time to rise up and destroy the enemy's works in your life.

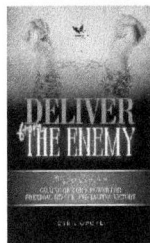

Deliver from the Enemy:

Calling on God's Power for Freedom, Rescue, and Lasting Victory

Break free from spiritual attacks and experience God's mighty deliverance in every battle.

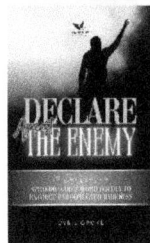

Declare Against the Enemy:

Speaking God's Word Boldly to Enforce Triumph Over Darkness

What if you could silence the enemy's schemes, protect your family, and walk boldly into every God-ordained assignment with unshakable authority?

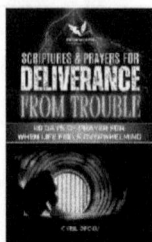

Scriptures & Prayers for Deliverance from Trouble:

40 Days of Prayer for When Life Feels Overwhelming

Are you walking through a season where life feels heavy and your prayers feel weak?

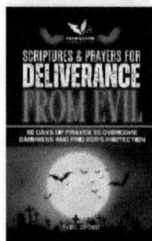

Scriptures & Prayers for Deliverance from Evil:

50 Days of Prayer to Overcome Darkness and Find God's Protection

When darkness presses in, how do you pray?

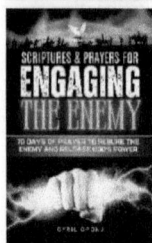

Scriptures & Prayers for Engaging the Enemy:

70 Days of Prayer to Rebuke the Enemy and Release God's Power

You weren't called to run from the battle—you were anointed to win it.

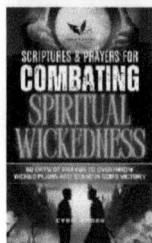

Scriptures & Prayers for Combating Spiritual Wickedness:

50 Days of Prayer to Overthrow Wicked Plans and Stand in God's Victory

Are you facing opposition that feels deeper than the natural? You're not imagining it—and you're not powerless.

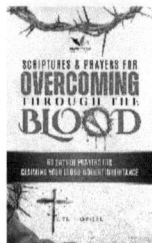

Scriptures & Prayers for Overcoming Through the Blood:

60 Days of Prayers for Claiming Your Blood-Bought Inheritance

You were never meant to fight sin, fear, or Satan in your own strength.

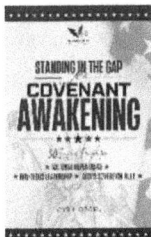

Standing in the Gap for Covenant Awakening:

30 Days of Prayer for National Repentance, Righteous Leadership & God's Sovereign Rule

What if your prayers could help turn the tide of a nation?

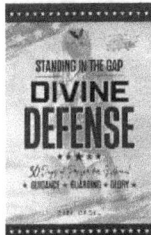

Standing in the Gap for Divine Defense:

30 Days of Prayer for National Guidance, Guarding & Glory

When the foundations of a nation feel as if they're shaking, prayer is the strongest fortress you can build.

Standing in the Gap for National Healing:

40 Days of Prayer for Reconciliation, Righteousness, and Restoration

What if your prayers could help heal a nation? What if God is waiting for someone—like you—to stand in the gap?

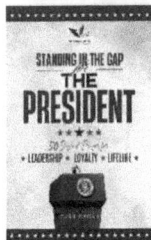

Standing in the Gap for The President:

50 Days of Prayer for Leadership, Loyalty, and Lifeline

When a nation's leader is under spiritual siege, will you answer the call to stand in the gap?

Pardon Through the Blood:

60 Days of Prayers for Total Forgiveness and Freedom

Guilt is a prison. The blood of Jesus holds the key.

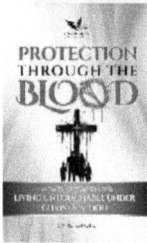

Protection Through the Blood:

60 Days of Prayers for Living Untouchable Under Christ's Blood

You are not helpless. You are not exposed. You are covered— completely—by the blood of Jesus.

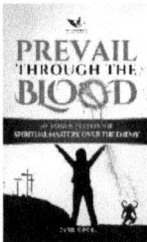

Prevail Through the Blood:

60 Days of Prayers for Spiritual Mastery Over the Enemy

What if every scheme of the enemy against your life could be dismantled—by one unstoppable weapon?

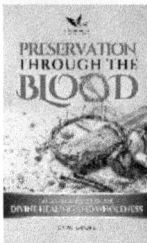

Preservation Through the Blood:

60 Days of Prayers for Divine Healing and Wholeness

Unlock Lasting Healing and Wholeness Through the Blood of Jesus

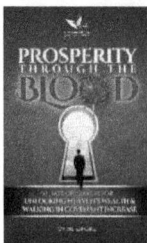

Prosperity Through the Blood:

60 Days of Prayers for Unlocking Heaven's Wealth and Walking in Covenant Increase

You were redeemed for more than survival—you were redeemed to prosper.

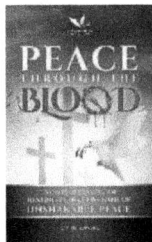

Peace Through the Blood:

60 Days of Prayers for Resting in the Covenant of Unshakable Peace

Are you ready to silence every storm of the mind, heart, and home—once and for all?